CHINA
A Personal Encounter with the People's Republic

CHINA
A Personal Encounter with the People's Republic

Text by Daniel Romualdez

Pictures by Philip Romualdez

PRENTICE HALL, INC.,
Englewood Cliffs, New Jersey

***China: A Personal Encounter
with the People's Republic***
**Text by Daniel Romualdez,
Pictures by Philip Romualdez**

Copyright © 1977 by Daniel Romualdez and Philip Romualdez

Art Direction and Design by Harold Siegel
Associate Designer: Linda Huber

Printed in the United States of America

Prentice-Hall International, Inc., London
Prentice-Hall of Australia, Pty. Ltd., Sydney
Prentice-Hall of Canada, Ltd., Toronto
Prentice-Hall of India Private Ltd., New Delhi
Prentice-Hall of Japan, Inc., Tokyo
Prentice-Hall of Southeast Asia Pte Ltd., Singapore
Whitehall Books Limited, Wellington, New Zealand

10 9 8 7 6 5 4 3 2 1

ISBN 0-13-132647-3

Library of Congress Catalog Card Number: 77-73646

Contents

Preface *vii*

Arrival in China *1*

Peking *7*

Tientsin *37*

Nanking *59*

Su-chou *89*

Shanghai *119*

Ch'ang-sha *145*

Canton *155*

While I was in the middle of a desperate struggle against spring fever in May of my sophomore year at Georgetown Prep, my father informed me that President Marcos was planning to make a state visit to China. The purpose of the trip was to open the process that would lead to the formalization of diplomatic relations between the Republic of the Philippines and the People's Republic of China. My father, who for some time had been serving as President Marcos's liaison to the Chinese government, told me that he would be participating in the upcoming talks. He invited me to tag along—in a completely unofficial capacity.

I arranged to take my last exam early. As soon as it was over, I flew home to Manila. My very precise schedule was ruined when the connecting flight from San Francisco to the Philippines was delayed for hours by engine trouble. As a result, I missed the plane that was taking the rest of the party to Peking. Luckily, I was still able to go on a backup plane, but of course I was hours behind everyone else. One thing I will always regret is the fact that because of my tardy arrival I missed the chance to see Chairman Mao even from a distance.

A few months later, when my father learned that government business would be taking him to China in August, he suggested that my brother and I take advantage of the opportunity to get to know China better. The plan was that my parents, my brother, and I would spend four or five days together in Peking. Then my mother and father would return to the Philippines, leaving my brother and me to travel around China on our own.

Unfortunately, duties at home shortened my parents' already brief visit to a mere two days. Nevertheless, my brother and I went on as planned, touring China on our own, accompanied by our Chinese guides and interpreters. We also were escorted by my father's male secretary, who was a pleasant companion and a refreshing reminder of home.

A year after the trip recorded in these pages, I was to visit China yet again, this time as the son of the first Philippine ambassador to the People's Republic. This was in the spring of 1976. We stayed in the embassy and had few opportunities to leave the confines of the diplomatic village, largely because Chou En-lai had just passed away and Peking was being rocked with the furor of the riots in Tien An Men Square.

Over that summer two tragedies hit China—the death of Chairman Mao and a massive earthquake. Both probably have changed the country dramatically. Some of the landmarks we saw in 1975 are no longer standing, and undoubtedly some of the attitudes and ideas we encountered are undergoing a transformation. Yet, perhaps because most of the people we met in China were young people of about our own age, I can't help but feel that the voices I heard are the voices of the future of China. At a time when the most populous nation on earth is in turmoil, and people everywhere are wondering what lies ahead, I consider myself fortunate to have had the opportunity to meet China's next generation.

ARRIVAL IN CHINA

As the plane descended cautiously on Canton, I pushed my forehead against the cold glass of the airplane window in my eagerness for a glimpse of the vast and verdant Chinese countryside. I could see coiled rivers wandering among the soft, gentle hills. I realized I was acting like a very inquisitive first-time tourist. Yet at the same time I felt I knew what to expect.

Actually, I had been to China only a few weeks earlier. Then I was a member of the official party of President Marcos on his first state visit to the People's Republic. Our reception was overwhelming, with battalions of applauding Chinese officials and an endless tableau of curious Peking faces as eager to catch a glimpse of the "foreigners" through our car windows as we were to get to know them.

But the rush of state business didn't permit us to stop. We drove on, past the rows of faces fading by the roadside.

This visit was going to be different. It was going to be a see-and-learn excursion in which my brother and I would see as much of China as we could cram into two busy weeks. Of course we planned to see the ancient cities and the beautiful temples that have attracted tourists since before the days of Marco Polo. But more important, we wanted to see the real China, where the Chinese people of today live and work. Most of all, I looked forward to meeting and talking with young people my own age. I hoped I would get to know them and, through them, China.

I stepped from the airplane into the piercing humidity of southern China's July heat. The Luxingshe guides who met us were natives of Kwangtung Province. Dark-skinned, short, and stocky, they reminded me of the inhabitants of Manila's Chinatown district. In fact, one of them, we soon learned, had lived in the Philippines before the war and spoke Filipino fluently.

While the customs and immigration people processed our papers—there is a lot of red tape in Red China—our hosts led us to the airport restaurant in the mammoth terminal. There were surprisingly few people in the airport, even for a weekday morning. Some tourists and businessmen milled about, but there was none of the bustle one usually finds at large airports. I couldn't help wondering why they needed such a large airport for so few people.

In the restaurant we were isolated in a tiny room separated from the public dining area by varnished plywood screens—an unnecessary courtesy, considering how few people were in the restaurant. We sat at a round table large enough to accommodate ten comfortably and were served by two pretty attendants wearing exactly the same uniforms as our hosts—narrow, blue cotton trousers and loose, short-sleeved cotton shirts.

Our lunch consisted of *dim sum*, pastries made of steamed wheat bread or rice pasta and stuffed with a variety of stewed meats and vegetables. This cuisine is very popular at home, so we were able to amuse our Chinese companions by trying to name each dish as it was served. Dessert was sliced watermelon, which our hosts ate with their hands. A bit unsure of ourselves, we used the Western fork and knife provided.

Watermelons, we were to find out later, were in season just then and we would see them everywhere. In the summer the Chinese eat watermelon for dessert or as a snack between meals. They even cut them in half and scoop out the fruit to make a sweet watermelon soup which is served in the hollowed-out shells. At city markets merchants piled stall after stall with them. Often we saw men and women crawling along the sidewalks to gather the fallen seeds, which are then dried and salted and eaten like candy. (At home, my brother and I have eaten more than our share of dried watermelon seeds, but after our trip I don't know that we will ever feel the same way about them again.) In China, where nothing is wasted, even the rinds are put to good use. The trucks that cart the watermelons to the city haul the rinds back to the countryside to be processed as feed for the pigs.

After lunch, we were led back through the Canton airport to reboard the plane for the flight to Shanghai, where we would stop briefly before going on to Peking. As we walked through the main lobby of the airport we passed a story-high portrait of Chairman Mao. A few minutes later we ran into him again in the waiting room, this time in the form of an oversized statue standing in front of a fluorescent red backdrop ornamented with quotations in gold characters.

4

A vegetable market in Peking

PEKING

It was late afternoon when we finally arrived in Peking. We were driven in a very comfortable Chinese limousine along a wide boulevard lined with thick-leafed shade trees set so close together that they formed a continuous canopy over us. Behind them an endless row of willows provided a second layer of insulation for the roadway. Our guide explained that the trees were not merely ornamental: they had been planted in order to contain the temperamental dust storms that periodically plague the arid city.

The drive into Peking is long and the rush hour traffic moved slowly. It didn't qualify as genuine "bumper-to-bumper" traffic because it consisted almost entirely of bicycles! Thousands of identical black bikes swarmed along the roadway, sometimes as thick as six abreast in each lane. In the city itself the broad main avenue has three lanes in each direction, but only one is reserved for automobiles. The others were packed handlebar to handlebar with darting bicycles. In addition, the sidewalks along the avenue, themselves as wide as highways, were filled with pedestrians ambling under the umbrella-like trees. The ornate street lights were just starting to come on as we approached our hotel. The lights, each consisting of almost a dozen white globes the size of basketballs, marched in a perfectly straight line all the way to the horizon.

The Peking Hotel is a conglomeration of three wings, each totally different from the others. We drove up an elevated driveway to the new wing, a seventeen-story high-rise. At the entrance, two automatic sliding glass doors flanked a large palm tree. Behind them was an immense lobby with ceilings high enough for a cathedral. In contrast, the upstairs corridor was dark and windowless and dimly lit.

WALKING TOUR

Before we had a chance to get settled, our guides arrived to tell us it was time for us to go to some acrobatic show. I wasn't really interested in acrobats at this point, so I tried to tell them I was too tired. My father, who was more direct, simply refused to go. At first the guides seemed distressed, but they knew my father from his previous trips to China and realized that his mind was set. My mother and brother, though, were willing to see the acrobats, so my father and I agreed to escort them to the car. Then, we said, we would go back upstairs to rest.

We saw them off but we didn't to back to our rooms as we had promised. Instead, I followed my father on a short walking tour of Peking, feeling both sly and triumphant at having escaped our well-meaning but demanding guides.

It was evening and the sidewalks were filled with people. I noticed something strange about the crowd but it took me a few minutes to realize what it was. There was an unusual orderliness in the way they walked, not in queues exactly, but in slightly regimented irregular lines. If my father hadn't noticed the same thing I might have thought my imagination was playing tricks on me, conditioned in part by all the things I had heard about Communist China.

Although the sidewalks were packed, people cleared a path

Handlebar to handlebar traffic

for us and gawked without embarrassment. Even in Peking foreigners are such a rare sight that the Chinese do not restrain their curiosity. Neither my father nor I was bothered by it, probably because we were so busy window shopping. I was finding out for the first time how normal their lives were. It seemed somehow exciting to realize that, for all our differences, they were basically just like us. They went shopping just as we did in stores that weren't all that different from what we had back home. Looking back now, I don't know what I expected, but at the time this minor revelation seemed profound.

BREAKFAST AND BANKING

Friday morning I woke up refreshed. Our accommodations were comfortable but austere. The only thing that caused excitement was the push-button curtains which opened up to a breathtaking view of the old Peking.

We had breakfast in a small dining room reserved for us—my father, my mother, my brother, my father's secretary, our two pilots and a mechanic, and myself. The meal was totally different from anything I'd ever had for breakfast. It consisted of an indescribable porridge, some cold chicken, a cold omelette served in slices, and a variety of chopped vegetables. I couldn't help thinking they were serving us leftovers. Being a habitual breakfast-skipper, I passed up everything. The shock was too much.

Because we were going out, our first order of business was to get our money changed. The bank in the lobby of the hotel was nothing more than a moderate-sized room; it looked like it had hardly any business to take care of. There wasn't even a guard. At first the only people we noticed working there were two young girls, one very businesslike, the other quite friendly, but then we saw, off in a corner, an elderly lady who was apparently a manager of some sort.

One of the girl tellers explained that the bank would not be able to change our Filipino money. Fortunately, my parents had some American money, which turned out to be acceptable. In order to change currency it was necessary to fill out a detailed form that reminded me of balancing my checkbook. At first the girl used an abacus to do her computing, but when the arithmetic got a bit complicated she pulled out a little Japanese calculator.

The forms made it clear that the Chinese didn't want us taking any of their money out of the country. They are even more strict about money than my parents are with me! The exchange rate was about one American dollar to two Chinese *yuan*. Their currency, which is superficially very complicated, is called *Renmin Ribao* or People's Money. The bills aren't decorated with portraits of heroes, but with pictures of everyday people in various work attire. The largest denomination available was a ten-*yuan* note, equal to about a five-dollar bill. I guess this reflects the austerity of their way of life. The Chinese normally do not spend large amounts of money. This is easy to understand because necessities are reasonably priced. To buy anything expensive, though, one practically needs a briefcase full of *yuans*.

10

THE FORBIDDEN CITY

As soon as we had finished our banking business, I joined my mother and brother who were led by a guide and an interpreter in a tour of the Forbidden City and the Temple of Heaven. We had to be driven in two gray Chinese-made sedans because regulations permit only one passenger in the front seat with the driver. As we drove through the city, I noticed that although all the government cars seemed to be Chinese or Russian makes, the taxis were Toyotas, Fiats, and even American cars. All the automobiles in Peking are either taxis or government cars. None is privately owned.

After the Great Wall, the Forbidden City and the Temple of Heaven are undoubtedly the major tourist attractions in all of China. Located in the heart of Peking, the Forbidden City is an elaborate walled compound that has housed the Chinese government for centuries. Its main gate, which is pictured on the seal of the People's Republic, faces Tien An Men Square and is guarded by the same oversize portrait of Chairman Mao that I had seen at the airports in Canton, Shanghai, and Peking.

The Imperial Palace, as it is also called, is a city in itself. Here, in a fortress island surrounded by a sea of slums, the emperor and his court used to live, insulated from the outside world by the massive crimson walls. Now some of the slums have been torn down to make Tien An Men Square, said to be the largest public square anywhere in the world, and the Forbidden City itself is no longer forbidden. Our guide kept emphasizing that today the people are free to pass through the gate and visit the old imperial city. This past-present comparison, I would soon learn, was one of the major themes of Chinese tour guides. Whenever they show you any of the beautiful treasures of their culture, they seldom resist making a political point about how terrible things were before the "Liberation."

Among the maze of buildings, those once used by the emperors themselves are distinguished by their golden tiled roofs. The tour included all the major buildings and soon began to bore us with an endless succession of throne rooms. We came to one room that was used for examining prospective members of the court. Even in ancient China, positions in the government and the court were awarded by competitive examinations—forerunners of the modern civil service exam.

As we wandered from room to room and building to building, I began to fantasize about the days when the Forbidden City *was* closed to the public, when princes strolled these grounds and the emperor dined on golden service, feasted on two-hundred course banquets, and napped during a hot summer afternoon on the coolness of woven ivory mats.

Even though I was captivated by the beauty of the objects on display, it was impossible not to agree with the point the guides kept making about the grotesque disparity between the royalty and the common people in the days of the Empire. The fact that a golden chest as tall as a man had been used to store the hair of an emperor's

Here the Emperor and his court used to live

A city in itself

Today the people are free to come through the gate and visit

Once in a while a Red Guard would scowl menacingly at my brother's lens

I began to fantasize about the days when princes strolled these grounds

mother was nearly obscene. The visual beauty of this gigantic vessel was undeniable, but either because of the propaganda of our guides or because of the sight of the modest and dowdy Chinese walking among these treasures, I couldn't help feeling uncomfortable and almost embarrassed by the vulgarity of such opulence.

Out on the grounds of the Forbidden City, Chinese children frolicked under the shadows of the gracefully curved roofs. Most of them seemed to be accompanied by only one parent, with mothers and fathers in about equal proportion. At the time I didn't understand why so few of the groups enjoying the day's outing were complete families, but a few days later I was to get the answer.

Meanwhile, my brother, the photographer in our family, was learning how camera-shy the Chinese are. For some reason they just do not like to be photographed. At the sight of his camera, men, women, and children would turn away or even flee. Once in a while a uniformed Red Guard would scowl menacingly at him. Luckily, he was able to find two small children who were willing to interrupt their play long enough to pose for pictures with us. Through an interpreter we had a few minutes of delightful, friendly conversation with them and with their grandfather, an elderly man with a long white beard. But when the old man tried to give us his address so that we could mail him the photographs, our guide interrupted and quickly crumpled the paper.

THE TEMPLE OF HEAVEN

From the Forbidden City we traveled a few miles to the Temple of Heaven. Consisting of three beautiful circular buildings with regal blue tiled roofs, the Temple stands in the middle of a green woodland on one of the highest hills in Peking. With a dramatic sneer, our guide explained that this is where the emperors used to pray.

The main temple is at one end of the clearing. From it, a paved formal promenade leads to a fenced-in courtyard. Here, if one whispers to the wall, someone directly on the other side of the wall can hear the words as distinctly as if he were next to the speaker. Beyond this courtyard is a terraced platform that continues the circular motif. Paved with an elaborate pattern of stones arranged in a complex order based on multiples of the number nine, this platform also exhibits the imperial court's fascination with acoustic tricks. If you stand at the center of the platform, your voice is magnified and projected outward exactly as if you were under a dome.

A CHINESE FEAST

After what seemed to be a long morning of sight-seeing, our guides brought us back to our hotel and told us we had a free afternoon. My mother decided to spend it shopping at the Peking Friendship Department Store and my brother and I elected to accompany her.

Most of the children seemed to be accompanied by only one parent

The department store is a four-story building located in the Diplomatic Village. On the first floor are the foodstuffs and the flower and garden shop. Upstairs, one floor is devoted to clothing, fabrics, furs, and shoes, while another sells household goods as well as bicycles, antiques, china, and jewelry. (The fourth floor is not open to the public.) Reserved exclusively for the use of the diplomatic community, the store was almost completely empty and for that reason much less interesting than the downtown department store I had seen with my father on our impromptu tour the night before.

After my mother finished her shopping, we returned to the hotel for a meeting with the man from the Foreign Office who was going to arrange our schedule. It turned out to be a short session in which my brother and I, aided by suggestions from a tourist booklet, told the man what we wanted to see. Even without his suggestions I had some ideas of my own and, in fact, had already prepared a typewritten list of cities I wanted to visit. This surprised the man from the Foreign Office; he said he would see what could be arranged, but made it clear he wasn't promising anything.

That evening the Foreign Office gave a banquet for us in a private dining room in the hotel. The two tables were filled with officials from the Chinese Foreign Office's Asian Department. At our table was the Chairman of Asian Affairs and Ke Hua, the Director of the Asian Department, a very formal man in a well-cut beige Mao suit who was soon to be named China's first ambassador to the Philippines. None of the Chinese had brought their wives, so the only women at the banquet, other than my mother, were government officials. They struck me as almost masculine in their manner and dress.

The banquet consisted of a lot of fine food, a great deal of toasting, and altogether too much fawning and flattery. But it was great fun and I was sorry we had to leave so early. My father had learned that afternoon that he would have to leave China the next morning on urgent business. My mother and father would be flying from Peking at dawn, and my brother and I were going to see them off at the airport.

ON OUR OWN

Before sunrise we motored to the airport in the boxy black Honji limousine. Although the city was still asleep, we did see a few individuals jogging and practicing shadow boxing, popular forms of exercise in China.

The airport was deserted at that early hour. In fact, my parents were not able to take off immediately because one of the people in charge of stamping the passports hadn't arrived yet! Some of the officials we had seen at the banquet the night before had come to see my parents off, so we chatted with them until it was time for my parents' plane to leave. I watched the jet take off with a strange feeling of rumbling emptiness in my gut. I felt excited yet apprehensive about what we would meet on our own in China.

PEKING ART AND HANDICRAFT FACTORY

In the afternoon we were driven to the Peking Art and Handicraft Factory in a remote section of the city. For the first time we ventured on streets that weren't wide avenues lined with trees. This was our first real glimpse of the residential part of Peking. Although it is certainly not unattractive, it is somewhat disappointing after the spacious elegance of the regal central portion of the city.

Along the way we passed some excavation for the already partially completed subway system. The trains would run along a route where the walls of the city once had stood; therefore, what was left of the wall had to be torn down to permit excavation and construction. Instead of digging a tunnel underground, we noticed, they were digging a deep, wide trench which then would have to be covered over. I am certainly no expert on engineering, but it seemed to me that the machines being used were not terribly modern.

The Peking Art and Handicraft Factory turned out to be a surprisingly small building. From the outside it looked more like it housed a small cottage industry than anything I associated with the word "factory." Yet there were 1,300 people, both men and women, working there, who produced nine different types of products. We were told that none of the many other craft factories in Peking had so many employees or made such a variety of goods.

At the entrance a blackboard bore a message in Chinese characters that, we were informed, meant, "Welcome to Our Friends from the Philippines." Before our tour could begin, we were led upstairs for a meeting with the manager of the factory, who proudly regaled us with an interminable verbal preview of what we were about to see. In the center of the room where we sat stood a large rectangular table suggesting a board meeting room. It was covered with a crowded arrangement of the factory's various products.

As we talked, cheerful attendants served steaming tea in covered porcelain mugs. The sweltering summer heat was not so much lessened as merely stirred around by the electric fans that dotted the ceiling. The room was almost as hot as the tea.

The manager explained that his establishment produced ivory carving, jade carving, cloisonné, filigree work, scroll paintings, lacquerware, lacquerware with gold wire inlay, "figures with flowers," and tiny glass bottles ingeniously painted on the inside. Their goods were exported to ninety countries throughout the world. He then went on to say that it was the factory's aim to produce traditional Chinese products "depicting good things in history and eliminating bad things." I didn't understand what he meant, but I was already beginning to get used to the fact that in China people never explain what they are doing without making reference to the Party line.

Our tour took us through the various workrooms, which were spacious but poorly lighted. The work is quite demanding, requiring great precision and intense concentration. For the most part the

workers use the traditional and rather primitive tools of their crafts. The one exception was the jade carving division, where there were machines to clean, polish, and even carve the semiprecious stones. The ivory-carving workroom was filled exclusively by old women using tiny hand tools that resembled dentists' drills.

I was told that the workers ranged in age from twenty to sixty, worked an eight-hour day, and were paid on a monthly basis. No one mentioned how much they earned and I was too embarrassed to ask.

On our way out of the factory I spotted some elephant tusks stored under a stairway. In answer to a question, our guide informed me that they came from Africa. It struck me as incongruous that the usually high-minded Chinese would do anything so ideologically decadent as killing elephants for dainty knickknacks. Many Western nations have already banned trafficking in ivory, and I was somewhat disappointed to learn that in China it is still a lucrative business.

Returning to the hotel for dinner, we entered the same enclosed dining room we had used with my parents. This time, instead of the large table for ten, the room held only a small table set for three. Dwarfed by the spacious room, the shrunken appearance of the table forced me to explode in laughter. Even the waiter snickered when he walked in and saw it. After dinner we told our guide that we wanted to give up the private room in order to eat with everyone else in the main dining room.

SUNDAY MASS

Motoring through bicycle-filled side streets on our way to Mass on Sunday, I noticed the city bustling with the activity of a normal workday. I asked our guide, Mr. Li, if working people were given Sunday off. Initially surprised by the question, he explained that most people worked a six-day week. Some had Sunday off, others had Monday, or Tuesday, or any of the other days. Now I understood why I had seen so many children in the Forbidden City accompanied by only one parent. In families where both parents work, I guess they don't often get the same day off.

As we talked, the car pulled up in front of a wooden gate in a massive gray concrete wall. This was the church. The building was old to the point of being decrepit. Inside it was dark, damp, and dusty. Only a few people were attending Mass, almost all of them foreigners, mostly from the African diplomatic community. Two elderly Chinese in Mao suits were the only local people in attendance. On a later visit I found out that they worked for the church. The Mass was celebrated by an aging Chinese priest in an ornate cassock. He said it in Latin, using the pre-Vatican II format in which he seemed to be mumbling in secrecy to himself.

A truckload of actors on their way to a performance

THE SUMMER PALACE

After Mass, we went off to the Summer Palace, where arrangements already had been made for my parents. Our guides decided that we might as well take advantage of the prior preparations even though my parents wouldn't be there.

The Summer Palace was first built in 1780, but the structure that now stands was newly rebuilt—a replica of the original, which was destroyed by fire. The beautiful estate, now open to the public, was filled with masses of people of all ages nonchalantly enjoying this once forbidden pleasure. Although they didn't say so explicitly, our guides hinted that the imperial compound had been turned into a public park in order to let the people see for themselves the gap that had existed between the rulers and the masses before the "Liberation."

In the center of the grounds a mammoth man-made lake sprawled endlessly, its waist-deep waters fed from the mountains that rise beyond the outskirts of Peking. The lake was dotted with dozens of tiny rowboats occupied by groups of teenagers, families, or even couples off by themselves. Usually one or two people were rowing while someone else held a parasol for shade from the blistering sun.

They seemed to be having loads of fun, so my brother and I started hinting to our hosts that we would like a boat ride. It turned out to be unnecessary, for we soon learned that it had all been arranged beforehand. Our guides led us down a covered outdoor corridor which was decorated on the ceilings and beams with thousands of miniature paintings, no two of which were the same. When we reached the lake front, the guides stopped to point out the marble boat that had been commissioned by Empress Tzu Hsi with money meant to be used to build a whole navy. Our interpreter kept repeating, "One boat for her instead of a navy for us."

We were given a small boat with a roof. As it was being shoved from the dock, some Chinese, apparently mistaking it for a public boat, tried to come on board. Our guides politely but firmly sent them off. They looked puzzled but did as they were told.

Out on the lake the air was filled with children's voices. They were enjoying themselves and, like children everywhere, they sang. When we asked what they were singing, our interpreter wrote out the lyrics for us in English. The song, as might be expected, was filled with propaganda about Chairman Mao and the joys of socialism.

Lest we get the impression that China was all ideology and no fun, our guide pointed to the far side of the lake where groups of teenagers were swimming. Swimming was not permitted anywhere in the lake, he explained, but the regulation was not enforced. Even the powerful Chinese Communist government, it seemed, wasn't about to try repressing the irrepressible spirits of youngsters at a lake on a hot summer day.

The lake was dotted with dozens of boats

A picnic under the covered promenade

PEKING DUCK

When we returned to the shore, we learned that it was too late for us to go on a tour of the Palace itself because reservations had been made for us in the Peking Duck Restaurant.

Located on a lightly trafficked side street, the restaurant was brimming with people. Fortunately, our reservation was for a private room. The restaurant turned out to be one of the few places we found in Peking that was air-conditioned. My brother and I both headed straight for the cold-air vents.

The meal started out with cold duck liver, which is not at all like pâté, and a number of other appetizers, all derived from various parts of the duck. We had to try everything. Then came the soup, which I assume was duck soup. Finally, a waitress brought in the main course, a succulent roasted duck, its skin a glistening golden brown. After we had looked at it admiringly for a few seconds, she took it back to the kitchen to be chopped. Other waitresses then brought out the crepe-like wrappers, the spring onions, and the sauce. When the duck returned, its dark brown meat had been cut into bite-size pieces and its crisp skin sliced into squares.

The procedure for eating Peking duck is to make little sandwiches consisting of a crepe, a piece of duck, a piece of skin, some sauce, and a spring onion. The spring onions, which have been scored across the bulb end and soaked in cold water, make a kind of edible brush which is used to apply the sauce to the duck. The crepe is folded more or less like a tortilla and eaten with the hands. It's a lot of fun and absolutely delicious.

After we thought we had eaten the whole duck, a small saucer was brought in. On it was the duck's head, sliced open with two surgically thin cuts. I was told that the brain was considered the best part. The idea didn't appeal to me, but after considerable urging I agreed to try it and was pleasantly surprised. I don't know if I'd say it was the *best* part, but the meat was firm and tasty. The meal ended with hot wash towels and, of course, watermelon.

SUBWAYS AND SOCCER

Later in the afternoon we went to see the Peking subway. Our guides already had obtained the special permits foreigners must show in order to enter the station. From something that was said I gathered that even the Chinese themselves cannot simply pay a fare and take a subway ride. They, too, must have permits to enter the station.

From the street level we walked downstairs to the platform. There are escalators but they only go up. As soon as we started down the stairs I noticed how clean everything was, but I didn't make much of it until I saw the all-marble station. It was absolutely immaculate.

The platform was crowded, but not uncomfortably so. In a few minutes a train arrived and we boarded it. Except for its cleanliness,

it wasn't very different from subway cars anywhere else. On the wall inside was a map of the route—a straight line with Chinese characters marking the stations. I couldn't help being struck by the fact that the car was filled to perfection, as though the flow of passengers was regulated by a computer. The effect was striking, especially in contrast to the always overcrowded busses. Our guides, I thought cynically, must have picked just the right time to take us on this tour. I'm sure there must be rush hours when the trains are jammed and other times when they run almost empty.

As we stopped in each station, I noticed a different colored marble plaque bearing the name of the station spelled out phonetically in Roman letters. Every station was as clean as the first one, and it wasn't hard to understand why the Chinese were so proud of their new subway system. After a very pleasant ride we returned to our hotel for a short rest.

In the evening we went to see a soccer match between a Chinese army team and Rwanda's national team. As we neared the stadium, which was located in the outskirts of the city, the streets became thick with traffic, filling the cool evening with a festive cacophony of bicycle bells and automobile horns. The sidewalks around the stadium were covered with thousands of parked bicycles.

We entered through a rear gate reserved for foreigners, all of whom had to sit in a special section. The stands were half empty when we came in, but gradually the stadium filled up. Then, as it got dark, the crowd thinned out again until, by the end of the game, the stadium was once again half empty. I can't imagine sports fans anywhere else in the world treating a soccer match like a cabaret act that you drop in on for a while and then leave when you have seen enough.

Before the game started, the two teams shook hands at midfield. The crowd seemed polite, neither noisy nor unduly quiet. But as the game progressed they grew more vocal and jeers mixed with the cheers. A voice over the public address system spoke constantly, and at one point my interpreter reported that it said something to the effect that it was only a game. According to his translation, one announcement said, "Our leader Chairman Mao has said, 'Winning friendship comes first, winning games is secondary.'" Even the patriotic PA, however, could not restrain the crowd when it disagreed with the referee's calls.

The Chinese team ultimately won, and the crowd was in an ebullient mood as it filed out of the stadium and headed for the bicycles. I was curious about how they would find their own bikes, which were all exactly alike, parked side by side. I never did find out.

As we neared the stadium,
streets became thick with tra

On Monday we were to leave Peking and begin our travels around China. The next ten days would take us to Tientsin, Nanking, Su-chou, Shanghai, Ch'ang-sha, Shao-shan, and Canton. We had enjoyed ourselves immensely in the Chinese capital, but there was so much else to see in the country that we were eager to be under way.

We set out early for the train station and then had a long wait because the train didn't leave until ten o'clock. Unlike the airports in China, the railroad stations are usually crowded, and one gets to see Chinese from all parts of the country. Although in China people tend to dress rather uniformly, it was easy to pick out the peasants, who looked starkly out of place among the hurrying masses on the platforms. They all seemed to be carrying as many of their belongings as their two hands and stooped frames could manage. Their faces were weathered, their clothes almost tattered.

Even though the trip to Tientsin would take only a few hours, we boarded a special sleeper car reserved for foreigners. In China it is often difficult to tell whether the special arrangements that are always being made for foreigners are a form of VIP treatment or a form of segregation. Did the government want to impress its guests by giving them the best accommodations, or did it merely want to prevent ideologically "impure" strangers such as ourselves from contaminating the people? I guess it's a combination of both.

The train moved rapidly, carrying us swiftly through the endless greenery of the Chinese countryside. It looked as I imagine it must have looked centuries ago, so rural, peaceful, and pastoral. Before we knew it, we were in Tientsin, where our passports had to be turned over for stamping by the local authorities. In China internal movement within the country is as strictly regulated as international travel is in the Western world. A foreigner needs a special permit to go anywhere out of the city limits of Peking, and the Chinese themselves are not allowed to establish residence outside of their native cities without permission from the government.

After the bureaucratic necessities had been taken care of, we were driven to our hotel. It didn't take more than a few minutes to see that Tientsin was a much older city than Peking. We drove down an old avenue flanked on both sides by rows of shoddy townhouses and massive stone banks. It was the way I pictured the London of Dickens' day in my imagination. The city exuded a charm and identity all its own. It is a pity that these buildings were destroyed in the earthquake the next summer.

Our hotel was an old building facing the park, but unfortunately our rooms were at the back overlooking an air shaft! Luckily, our schedule was busy enough to keep us from having to spend too much time in them.

EAST IS RED
MIDDLE SCHOOL

After lunch and a short rest, we motored to the Tung Fang Huang (East Is Red) Middle School. As soon as we pulled into the driveway, we noticed that it was lined with students who immediately began

It looked as I imagine it must have looked centuries ago

clapping and shouting a welcome. I realized they only wanted to give us a warm greeting and to make us feel welcome, but I found it quite embarrassing to be treated in this way by kids my own age.

We were greeted at the door to the main building by the headmaster, Mr. Wang Chung-ling. He led us to a reception room, where he presented a brief account of the school. A middle school, he explained, is roughly equivalent to a combined junior high and high school in Western countries. Tung Fang Huang Middle School has 1,598 students and 130 full-time teachers. The campus area occupies approximately 12,000 square meters. Buildings take up more than half this space.

He told us that in the feudal system that existed in China before the "Liberation," few young people could afford to go to school. "The Chinese Communist Party instituted a system of universal education," he proudly proclaimed, "so now all school-aged children go to school. Nevertheless, up until the Proletarian Cultural Revolution, education was divorced from political ideology and productive labor. Then the Cultural Revolution transformed our educational system. Workers' propaganda teams began coming to the schools to implant the Party's belief that education must be in step with the policies of the proletariat and must combine with productive labor in order to train students so that they will develop into workers who will advance both the policies and the culture of socialism."

He went on and on in the same vein, like a cross between a political orator and a proud schoolmaster advertising his school to a prospective student. He told us that in the first year in middle school each student studies Chinese language, mathematics, politics, a foreign language, agricultural machinery, geography, history, music, and fine arts. The next year physics is added to the curriculum, and in the third year chemistry is added to the already heavy load. In senior middle school each student must take one year of Japanese and two years of English.

He explained that the school followed the teachings of Chairman Mao, who had proclaimed that education must learn from industry and agriculture. Toward this end the Tung Fang Huang Middle School had sent students to ninety-six different factories in the Tientsin area so that they could learn about industry firsthand. In addition, it had a staff of 116 peasants, workers, and soldiers who served as part-time teachers.

"I am sure you realize it is now summer vacation," he said, "but our school is not closed. On the contrary, our students have organized themselves and are taking part in various activities that will help them implement the Party's ideals and will aid in their moral, intellectual, and physical development. They have invited advanced workers to give lectures and to teach them the good ideology of serving the people. So you see, in this way they make worthy use of their summer vacation. They have a beneficial rest and at the same time advance their development."

I wasn't sure I did see. It all sounded rather forced and artificial to me. I couldn't imagine kids my own age wanting to "make worthy

use of their summer vacation" by studying "the good ideology of serving the people." In fairness, though, it may be that the stilted English of the interpreter made it sound worse than it was.

At the end of his little lecture Mr. Wang pointed out that the methods used in his school were still in the experimental stage. He said that after we had toured the school he would be glad to hear any suggestions we had. I felt very flattered but I didn't get the impression he said it merely to flatter us. Somehow it convinced me that this man was very sincere about wanting to develop a good school.

The first stop on our tour was the chemistry lab. It was an advanced lab that gave clear evidence of the emphasis on the pragmatic element in Chinese education. The students were conducting experiments with fertilizers and assorted agricultural crops. Similarly, in the electricity class they were studying problems related to the generation of power for irrigation. For our benefit they did a simple demonstration, lighting a string of electric bulbs with power from a generator they had built.

Some of their activities weren't quite as impressive as what I saw in the science classes. In the foreign language class two students put on a mock telephone conversation in English. Honestly, I thought they were speaking Chinese! It took me a few minutes to realize that the strange sounds I was hearing consisted of English words.

Our next stop was the acupuncture class—really the infirmary. The wall was covered with charts and the room was filled with students practicing on themselves. We asked one girl, who had a needle between her eyebrows and others in her arms and legs, if it was painful. She smiled and said it wasn't. From the little I could understand, it seemed that for a headache the needle is stuck in the arm whereas for a stomachache it is stuck in the foot, or something of that sort. It was bizarre.

From the infirmary we went to the recreation hall, where of course the most prominent space was given over to the Ping-Pong tables. My brother Philip, who is considered a pretty good player at home, wanted to give it a try. I think he was a little disappointed when our guide selected a seven-year-old child to be his opponent. To his chagrin, the little tyke simply massacred him.

After we left the recreation area, we paused to peek into a room where students were giving each other haircuts under the supervision of a professional barber. They offered to cut our hair, but as soon as Philip heard that he rushed out. I quickly followed him to the handicraft class. It reminded me of our work education class in Manila, except that they seemed so much more skilled than we were. I wondered why they could do everything so well.

Our last stop was the discussion class. The students are divided into four groups and their discussion is led by a soldier and a peasant who serve as moderators. The purpose of the class is to guide the ideological development of the students. Every day each student writes in his or her diary what he has done that day "to answer the call of Chairman Mao." Then these diary entries become the subjects of the discussion. It struck me as a sophisticated form of brainwashing

TAGANG OIL FIELD

Tuesday morning began with a long mesmeric drive down a narrow road flanked on both sides by fields of grain. Suddenly the scenery changed and the land, which ages ago had lain under the ocean, was barren and flat. Brown mud stretched before us as far as we could see, with here and there a vertical eruption of flame where natural gas leaked from the earth. We were in the Tagang Oil Field.

We drove along a network of paved roads that appeared out of nowhere. Finally we pulled to a stop in front of a one-story building in a fenced-in yard. We went inside and met Mr. Tou, who would give us an introductory speech about the oil field.

Drilling began in December of 1964, after a geological survey predicted that large pools of oil could be found under the mud fields. In 1950 American specialists had reported that there was no oil in Northern China, and a few years later Russian experts had declared that any attempt to start an oil field in the Po Hai Gulf area was doomed to failure. Trusting their own survey, the Chinese began to drill, hoping for a chance to prove the United States and the Soviet Union wrong. Within a year they had found oil.

At first there were only 8,000 workers at the Tagang Oil Field and living conditions were extremely bad. In fact, the original workers had to transport all their own equipment—over 10,000 tons of it— from other oil fields before they could begin work. There were no houses for them, no fresh food, no electricity, and no oil for their lamps. "But because of their adherence to the teaching of Marxism-Leninism and the writings of Chairman Mao, and because of their self-reliance and willingness to undergo a hard struggle in order to produce the economic resources necessary for building socialism, the oil field was developed very quickly."

Today there are 20,000 workers in the Tagang Field, many of them women. Their average age is only twenty-two and their living conditions are greatly improved over those of the original pioneers. "Of course," Mr. Tou concluded, "there are still imperfections, such as the waste of materials. But our workers are determined to carry on the spirit of hard struggle and self-reliance. They will speed up the pace of construction of the oil field because in this way they can make their contribution to Chairman Mao's socialist revolution."

When the briefing session was over, we boarded an olive green military jeep and drove to an oil-extraction station. A young male worker showed us a complicated diagram of how the station worked. He said that his station produced 110 tons of oil a day, reaching down 2,600 meters below the surface to get it. Then he started the mechanism. After a few minutes of desperate noise, a tube started spitting out a thick gooey black substance. We watched the crude oil collect for a few minutes and then continued our tour.

At our next stop we were introduced to a seventeen-year-old female worker. She said she had been at the oil field for about six months, along with twelve classmates from her school. We asked her whether she found it lonely, being separated from her family, and

A farm in Tientsin

Tagang oil field

she assured us that she didn't. She quickly added that this was because her parents had been able to visit her a few times and because she boarded with her former classmates. We didn't get to find out very much about the kind of work she did because most of our time with her was spent answering her questions. She was very curious about us and about young people in other parts of the world.

We then boarded our jeep again for a ride along the slushy road to an oil storage station. The station was managed by twelve women. When I asked whether there were any men working there, one of them answered, "Mao's directive says that times have changed and now women can do whatever men do." That certainly answered my question!

One of the women explained that their job was to maintain the equipment in the station. They hadn't received any special training but had learned everything they needed to know on the job. She said that the station consisted of four tanks and that all of the equipment was made in China.

All of the women were very friendly and didn't seem to mind answering questions. Miss Shen said she was twenty years old and more or less in charge of the others. Miss San was twenty-three and Miss Gi twenty-four. They worked three shifts with four women to a shift. Miss Shen said that the average worker had been at the fields for about three years and that most of them came from Tientsin or the nearby countryside. Because of their heavy work schedule, though, they got to go home only once a year when they had their vacations. She also managed to get in the fact that many foreigners had come to inspect the station and they always had words of praise for the good management.

Like most of the workers I was to meet, she seemed to enjoy her work and to take great pride in it. Sometimes it seemed to me that they had been brainwashed into thinking there is no greater pleasure than serving the state. But on the other hand, they really seemed to like what they were doing and sounded sincere in what they said. After talking with them I always went away with mixed feelings.

From the storage station we were driven back for lunch in the little building where we had met Mr. Tou. While we were eating, a heavy rainstorm swept across the field and forced us to cancel the rest of our tour. To make up for it, Mr. Tou arranged for us to have a discussion with four workers. As soon as we had finished eating, we were taken to a reception room and introduced to two young women —Chen Chi, twenty-two, and Wang Yan-min, twenty-one—and two young men—Li Lian-yin, twenty, and Chang Kuan-shun, twenty-two. They told us to ask any questions we wanted and promised to answer them to the best of their ability. An older man, apparently their supervisor, was also present.

Miss Chen said she was from Tientsin. Miss Wang came from a nearby rural area. She said that her parents also worked in the oil field but that she did not live with them. Of the two young men,

It struck me as rather a bold question, and apparently it struck their superior the same way. He interrupted immediately, before I could answer, and said that young people in China take Political Studies, which teaches them how to serve the people. "This is why Chen, for example, is always ready to answer the call of the state," he said. He added that of course young people in China had preferences, but their highest preference was always to render service to the state and to the people. "With individual preferences come contradictions and indecision," he concluded, "and so, in order to avoid this, it is better to listen to what the state wants you to do."

To me it sounded like a feeble argument but I didn't think it was my place to say so.

There was an awkward silence, which Miss Chen smoothed over by volunteering to tell us about their work schedule. "We get up at six o'clock for military exercises," she said, "because everybody here is in the militia. Then we have breakfast at six-thirty and start work at seven-thirty. We have lunch at twelve."

Without any warning, the superior suddenly erupted like a volcano. "As long as there are imperialists in the world," he declared, "there are enemies, and so there is a need to have militiamen who are workers during peacetime and soldiers in war."

I was amazed, but Miss Chen, unfazed, continued. "During our lunch break we do calisthenics and listen to the radio. Then we go back to work at two-thirty. At six o'clock we finish work for the day. In the evening we chat with our friends or do whatever we want. I usually like to do some political reading. We usually go to bed between nine-thirty and ten."

At this point my brother Philip took a turn at questioning them. "Do you ever go dancing?" he asked.

Miss Chen: Only folk dances. Many young people prefer to sing Peking Opera songs or patriotic songs.

Philip: Do you use cosmetics?

Miss Chen: No. (She giggled, then added:) Sometimes, when we go out to a performance, we use a little perfume.

Philip: What about hair styles?

Miss Chen: The women either wear their hair short or wear pigtails if their hair is long.

Philip: What about the men? How come no one has hair like us? (My hair was fairly long at the time and Philip's was very long.)

Mr. Chang: Style of hair depends upon the convenience it will allow the person.

Philip: Do any of the men wear mustaches?

Mr. Chang: It is allowed. There are no restrictions. But it is not very popular with young people.

Philip: I noticed that most of the women were wearing pants. Is that what you wear all the time?

Miss Chen: No, sometimes we wear dresses. We usually prefer dresses when it's very hot.

Philip: I was wondering, if you don't get to pick what you want to do, doesn't that make you less motivated to work?

Mr. Li: No. On the contrary, we work even more actively because we are working for the people.

Supervisor: Sometimes they even have to be persuaded to take a rest because otherwise they just keep working without stopping. You see, when a person is in middle school he fills out an application in which he can declare the kind of government assignment he is interested in. These preferences are taken into consideration when assignments are made. Of course in some cases people are not assigned in accordance with their preferences, but you can always use your spare time to pursue your interest. For example, if a person is interested in cultural things, he can join the propaganda movement in the factory. They put on performances and have poetry readings and other things of that nature.

At this point our interpreter from the Foreign Office, Mr. Li, suggested that we end the discussion because we were running behind schedule.

On our way back to Tientsin we passed an oil rig. Even after my day in the oil fields it still looked strange to me. In my mind I associated oil rigs with Texas, not China.

We had a quick dinner in Tientsin and then rushed to catch our train back to Peking, where we would spend the night before flying on to Nanking in the morning. The rain hadn't let up all afternoon, and some of the streets in Tientsin were so badly flooded that water began to leak in through the floorboards of our car. When it stalled in the middle of a particularly deep puddle, I was certain we were going to miss our train. Fortunately, whole families had gathered in the doorways of their homes, drawn by the strange sight of a car full of stranded foreigners. Suddenly half a dozen men came out into the rain and cheerfully pushed us to higher ground. Then they disappeared without even waiting to be thanked.

We made it to the train station just in time and were pleasantly surprised to learn that we wouldn't have to travel in a special section for foreigners. We rode in one of the regular cars filled with Chinese. As luck would have it, the people next to us were a middle-aged Chinese couple from New York who were spending a month in China visiting relatives.

*Whole families had gathered in
the doorways*

→

The car and truck traffic was as light as the railroad traffic was heavy

←

Nanking waterfront

A monument commemorates the
self-reliance and perseverance
that built the Nanking bridge

Lower level, Nanking Yangtze
River Bridge

We were surprised to see a crowd of tourists

They were right. When we got to the top, the first thing we saw was the same group of Americans we had met at the mausoleum. I wondered aloud whether the Chinese give everyone the same tour, prompting the Americans to ask us about our plans. It turned out that our itineraries were not really identical, although they were going to be in Shanghai the same day we were. We joked about running into them there and then made our way to the balconies for a glimpse of the view we had worked so hard to get.

Before us the thickly forested hills stretched as far as we could see in every direction. It was a breathtaking sight. As I scanned the horizon, my eye was arrested by a brilliant blue patch in the middle of the woods. Gleaming like a sapphire set in jade, the tile roof of the Sun Yat-sen Mausoleum reminded us of where we had just been.

NANKING TEACHERS' COLLEGE

Our schedule that afternoon called for a visit to the Nanking Teachers' College. We were met at the entrance by Mr. Ding, the chairman of the college's Music Department. He conducted us to his office, pausing along the way to point out the intricate carved pillars, the ornate windows, and the tasseled lamps that ornamented the traditional-style building. The only modern touches were the huge electric fans that hung from the ceiling.

"Before the Liberation," Mr. Ding informed us, "the school was known as Ching-ling Course College and had an enrollment of about one hundred students from wealthy families. Today we have over four thousand students who represent all elements in our society. We have dedicated ourselves to the task of assisting in the consolidation of the dictatorship of the Chinese proletariat. Toward this end we emphasize the ideological education of our students, working continuously to heighten their political consciousness. We also have reformed our admission procedures. Before the Proletarian Cultural Revolution our students were all selected directly from the middle schools. Now we also admit a great many soldiers and workers who are able to bring to their education the benefits of their practical experience. In fact, all our students are required to augment their classroom work with practical knowledge in such fields as industrial work, farming, military affairs, and criticism of the bourgeoisie."

Mr. Ding further explained that in addition to the work done at the school itself, there is an extensive correspondence program that enables the college to spread its benefits among workers, soldiers, and farmers in rural areas and other remote parts of the country. "In this way," Mr. Ding boasted, "we are complying with Chairman Mao's 'May Seventh Directive' in which he said that the school should be seen as an open doorway."

At the conclusion of Mr. Ding's introductory speech, we were taken to see the Fine Arts Department, which was the only one of

Our elderly guide surprised us by speaking English with an American accent

the school's eleven departments actively functioning during the summer vacation. The Art Department was located in one of the relatively modern buildings I had noticed on the campus. We were greeted at the door by an old man with a thick white moustache and thinning white hair. He surprised us by speaking English with an American accent, a rarity in China, where the few people who speak English usually do so with British accents.

He led us up a flight of stairs and down a long corridor hung with brightly colored paintings, the work of students at the school. I noticed that in style and subject matter they were just like the propaganda posters one sees all over China, but I thought it best to keep this observation to myself since I didn't know how it would be taken.

At the end of the corridor we went into a small studio where some of the school's teachers were working on water color scroll paintings in the traditional style. We watched them for a while, impressed by the meticulousness of their work, which was a copy of an ancient painting. Our elderly guide then asked if we would like to see a display of calligraphy techniques. When we said we would, the old man said a few words in Chinese to a faculty member who was standing by a drawing table. The calligrapher took a few seconds to prepare his well-used horsehair brush. Then he began covering a piece of rice paper with the dizzyingly intricate strokes of Chinese characters. Even without knowing much about the technique, we were able to appreciate his tremendous skill as he manipulated the brush, mixing pencil-thin lines with broad black strokes. He did it all in what seemed a matter of seconds, taking more time after he had finished to stamp the paper with his own personal seal—the equivalent of the artist's signature in Western paintings. Then he cleaned his brush and carefully replaced it in a receptacle on his desk.

"I know you would like to talk to some students," our elderly guide said, "but I'm afraid you are going to be disappointed. In the summer there are very few students here. But perhaps we shall be lucky."

With that, he led us on a brief search of the building which turned out to be quite successful. We managed to find a few students who were gracious enough to take the time to talk to us. I think the things they had to say were quite interesting, for they provide a good insight into the attitudes and feelings of the young generation of educated Chinese.

Tung Wan-shan, a young man in his early twenties, told us:
I graduated from Middle School in Wu Hsi in 1969. Acting on Chairman Mao's call to educated young people to go to rural areas and integrate themselves with the workers and the peasants, I went to join the production corps of the People's Liberation Army in the northern part of Shansi Province. We were organized in platoons, just like in the Army. My platoon mainly engaged in agricultural production. We grew rice, wheat, and cotton. We also continued our studies in the field while we were working.

I stayed in the construction and production corps of the PLA for five years. Then I decided to apply for admission to the Teachers' College. After I submitted my applications, my comrades in the platoon discussed whether or not I was qualified to be recommended to be a student at the college. Then they submitted a recommendation to the leadership of the construction and production corps of the Chinese People's Liberation Army in northern Shansi Province. This is how I came to be here. When I have completed my education I would like to return to northern Shansi Province, but I don't think this is likely because, generally speaking, the students here at the Teachers' College will be assigned to teach in the middle schools or to some other post as recommended by the Party or the government. If I can return to northern Shansi I will be very happy, but if I am sent elsewhere I also will be happy to be of service to the cause of socialist construction.

After he had finished speaking, a young female student from Su-chou told us her story. Her name was Wang Chu-chen and this is what she had to say:

I graduated in 1969, and in response to Chairman Mao's call I too settled down in the northern part of Shansi Province. At the time I was only seventeen years old. There were four of us and at first I had a lot of difficulties. But we were treated quite well by the poorer peasants. When we arrived, the house where we were supposed to stay wasn't ready for us, so we just lived with the peasants. They were very kind to us and treated us like their own children.

Being born in the city, I had no idea of how much physical labor was involved in farm work. At the beginning the peasants were very patient with us. I had arrived there in the wintertime, which is when the peasants collect the manure and carry it to the fields. Because I had never had to carry things on my shoulders in the city, my shoulders became swollen and at night I felt so much pain that I almost cried. Then many of the peasants came to see me and told me how to carry things on my shoulders so that it wouldn't hurt. This taught me how important it is not to have intellectual airs. You have to be willing to learn from all people, especially the workers and the peasants.

In addition to our work on the farms, we went to political studies classes where we were taught about the history of the family and the history of the village so that we would be able to make comparisons between the past and the present. This education brought about great changes in our ideology and our feelings and we no longer had any difficulty getting used to working and studying together with the poor peasants.

In 1972 a primary school was set up in the village and the peasants recommended me as a teacher. At first I didn't like the idea of being a primary school teacher because I wasn't interested in being with small children so much. But after a while I realized that doing educational work was a very important way to make a contribution to socialist construction. When I realized this, I applied to the Teachers'

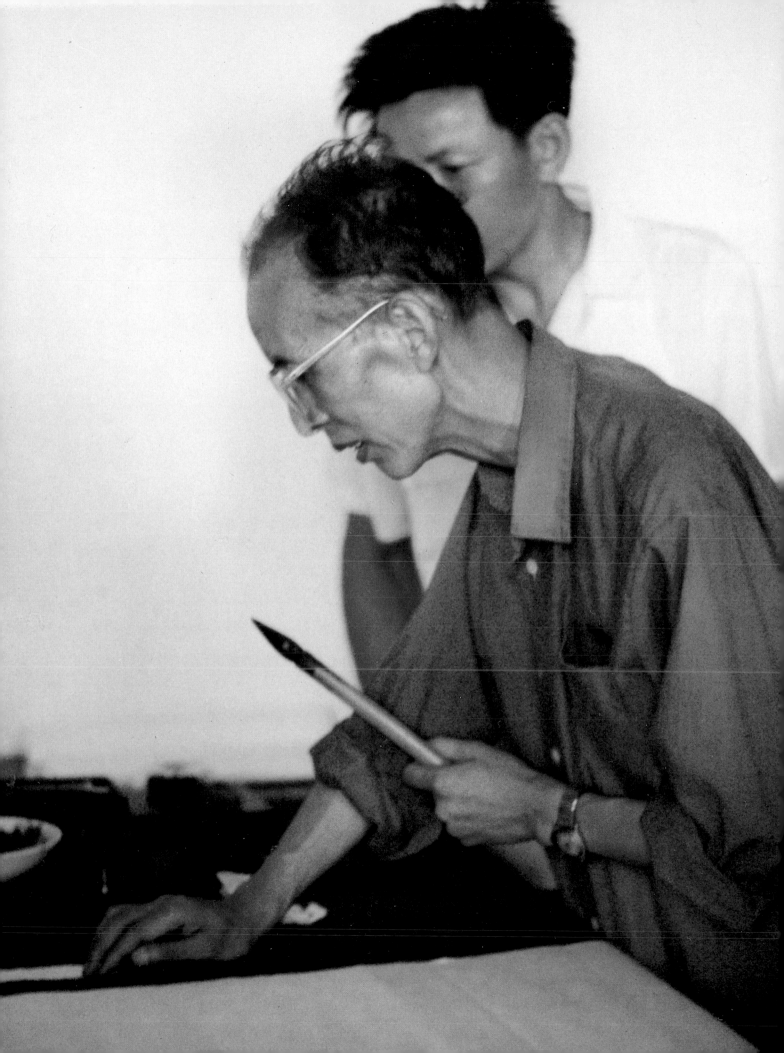

College and my application was endorsed by the peasants and the leadership of the local Party committee. I came to the college last year and now I am studying in the Music Department.

I emerged from our conversations with Tung Wan-shan and Wang Chu-chen somewhat confused. When I first started speaking with young Chinese people I found their overwhelming altruism rather refreshing, perhaps only because it was a change from the preoccupation with ourselves which characterized the young people I knew at home—including myself. But after a while it began to get on my nerves. The constant talk about "answering the call of Chairman Mao" and "assisting in the cause of socialist construction" was decidedly unnatural, and I longed to hear one of them complain that his or her own desires weren't taken into consideration. Instead, I couldn't even get them to admit that they had desires of their own. It is one thing to give up what you want to do in answer to a "higher" duty, but it's quite something else not to even let yourself have preferences.

Yet, as Wang Chu-chen told her story, I thought I detected a note of subdued protest. Everything she said followed the Party line, but something in the way she talked hinted that she had learned this kind of obedience only after a long struggle with herself. When she told me that as a result of her "political studies classes" she "no longer had any difficulty getting used to working and studying together with the poor peasants," I was both inwardly pleased and saddened. It was somehow reassuring to hear that she had had "difficulties" when she was uprooted from her home in the city and sent to work on a farm. Her words reminded me that behind all these selflessly idealistic young people were kids with attitudes and preferences, likes and dislikes, just as one finds anywhere else in the world. The difference, of course, was that these young people were being taught that such things aren't supposed to count.

MEETING AT THE BRIDGE

When we got back to the guesthouse, we were informed that a meeting had been arranged for us that evening with a group of young people. Having just come from interviewing the students at the Teachers' College, we weren't looking forward to more "work" that day. But when our guides explained that the meeting would be held at the top of the Nanking Yangtze River Bridge and that the bridge lights, normally used only for ceremonial occasions, would be turned on for our benefit, we became quite excited.

We rushed through dinner and then hurried back upstairs to our rooms, my brother for his camera and I for my tape recorder. We were ready to leave a half hour before our driver showed up with the car.

The bridge, which had been very impressive in the afternoon, was breathtaking at night. The lights appeared to trace a waltzing

The bridge lights were turned on for our benefit

fact, sometimes the peasants have excellent knowledge about how to treat common illnesses such as colds, coughs, and stomachaches. The barefoot doctors do not discourage this ancient method of treatment. We try to combine traditional Chinese medicine with modern Western techniques.

The important thing to remember is that we generally put prevention of disease before cure. We have a very thorough program of innoculation against such diseases as encephalitis and malaria, which used to be prevalent in the area where I am working. We also teach the people hygiene and other aspects of health care.

In addition to working on the farms and practicing as a barefoot doctor, I am also a deputy to the National People's Congress. I don't have any specific job in the Congress, but I attend the meetings as the representative of the peasants where I live. That is to say, I am more or less a bridge between the masses and the government. I think it is a very good thing that a person in my position can serve in this way, because as a result, the health needs of the people can be made known to the government.

When she stopped speaking I told her I was very impressed with what she had told me about the barefoot doctors. The system seemed like an excellent way to get health care to people who otherwise wouldn't be able to receive it. "You should be very proud of the work you are doing," I said.

She smiled and answered, "I believe that we do good work. But we must be modest and prudent and must learn to serve the people still better."

*A luminous red flag hung in the
night like fireworks*

Early Friday morning we said good-bye to the guesthouse staff and drove to the Nanking railroad station. The sun was just coming up when we got there. At first we were the only people on the platform, but soon others arrived and before long the station was bustling with travelers.

We boarded the train and found ourselves in a comfortably appointed car with deep brown paneling and two rows of upholstered chairs with antimacassars facing each other. Between them was a table decorated with potted flowering plants.

Through the door at the end of the car we could see that the next car was completely filled with foreigners of all nationalities— a miniature version of the United Nations, except, of course, for the fact that there was no provision for simultaneous translation. We could hear shouting in at least half a dozen different languages. Off to one side, a portly African man in elaborate robes was chanting something, while a few feet away the strident strains of an Arabian melody were blaring from a portable cassette recorder. In the distance a small group of Italians was singing and all the while a high-pitched voice was squealing something over the public address system in Chinese.

The spectacle was so fascinating that I couldn't resist the temptation to get a closer look. I pushed open the door and walked into the car, feeling as though I had been suddenly thrust into the middle of some exotic bazaar in Casablanca. When I had made my way through to the other side of this car full of foreigners, I noticed that the next car was filled with Chinese. Hoping for a chance to talk to some of them, I tried the door, only to find that it was locked. I laughed to myself, unable to decide in my own mind whether the foreigners were being locked in or out. Then, not yet willing to go back to my own seat, I found a group of young Italians who were studying at the Peking Foreign Language Institute and struck up a conversation with them.

The trip passed quickly, thanks to a lively chat with Maria Laura, a young Italian student who kept mixing French and Chinese phrases into her animated English.

We arrived in Su-chou at noon. There my brother and I were met by guides who drove us to the guesthouse where we were to stay. Like the guesthouse in Nanking, this one was also a grand old mansion that the Revolution had transformed into a hotel. My room overlooked a stone sculpture garden and a large man-made pond. I was soon to learn that Su-chou is celebrated for this style of landscape gardening.

Our room had a feature I had never seen before. We were provided with an ice bucket well stocked with individually wrapped ice cubes. The Chinese almost never drink cold beverages, even in the south, where the heat is often unbearable. Indeed, on the day we arrived, Su-chou was steaming like a furnace and just then a glass of ice water seemed more tantalizing than the most elaborate Chinese banquet ever could have been. My brother and I unwrapped enough ice to fill two glasses and quickly drank our fill.

90

Tiger Hill Garden

The gardens of Su-chou

"This is our Tower of Pisa"

Su-chou. A small private estate before the Revolution, it was now one of the most cozy and elegant parks I have ever seen, with delightful landscaping, a pond that dominated the property, and a few fascinating optical illusions. One of its most interesting features was a mirror that looked like a window. The glass was set into it in such a way that even if you were directly across from it, you would not see your own reflection. Apparently it dates back to the Ch'ing Dynasty.

Our guide surprised us by refraining from exploiting it for propaganda purposes. In fact, she seemed to take a genuine delight in all the gardens of Su-chou—a fact which may explain why we saw so many of them. Not once did she say so much as a word about the decadence of life under the emperors.

TUNG TING PEOPLE'S COMMUNE

On Saturday morning we drove to Tung Ting People's Commune, which occupies seventy square kilometers of land along the edges of Tai Hu Lake. Its population of 46,000 is divided into thirty production brigades and 230 production teams. Although it is situated on the waterfront, its economy is diversified. It grows rice and fruits, harvests fish, maintains a carving industry and a marble quarry, and also produces *pilochun* tea. (*Pi* means jade green, the color of the tea; *lo* means conch, the shape the spiral tea leaves approximate; and *chun* means spring, the season when the leaves are ready to be picked.) The fruits grown at the commune from March until November include strawberries, peaches, and oranges, as well as walnuts, ginkgo nuts, and chestnuts. Fishing is done both in Tai Hu Lake and in the numerous fish ponds that occupy a large portion of the grounds. Another source of livelihood in this sprawling commune is silk weaving, which accounts for a fifth of the commune's total income.

The commune was founded in 1958 after Chairman Mao issued a call for more grain production. Over the years, the commune has made great progress. Its members have built hundreds of kilometers of roads and many miles of embankments to prevent flooding from the lake. They also have erected dozens of pumping stations in order to utilize water from the lake to irrigate the hilly areas.

Mr. Wang, the head of the commune's Revolutionary Committee, told us that one of the reasons for the commune's constantly increasing productivity is the ability of its workers to combine practical knowledge with intellectual innovation. Toward this end, the commune, which includes 700 young middle school graduates among its population, has developed a system in which each production brigade contains its own agricultural research group. These groups always include both peasants and young people so that the practical experience of the former can be merged with the

One of the most cozy and elegant parks I have ever seen

Commune members have built
hundreds of kilometers of roads →

← Tai Hu Lake

Dining Hall attendants, Tung Ting People's Commune

Children of the commune

usual manner while the other circulates among the students as a sort of coach. The coaching, though, does not seem to concern the subject matter of the class: the purpose of the second teacher is to supervise the ideological development of the students. It seemed to me a rather bizarre system, but the students with whom I spoke accepted it as natural.

At one point I made the mistake of asking whether there were any sex education classes at their school. Before any of the students could answer, the woman who was interpreting for us said brusquely, "We have health education classes but we don't pay too much attention to sex." She said it in a very condescending way, and after that I got the distinct impression that she was less friendly to us than she had been.

A CHINESE HOME

After our talk with the young people, we were taken to visit the home of a leader of one of the production brigades. The man of the house was not at home but his wife was kind enough to show us around. The house had two bedrooms, which would have been rather crowded for her family of six were it not for the fact that the two older children had moved away from home. When I noticed that there was no kitchen and no stove anywhere in the house, I asked her where she did her cooking. She explained that she and her family used to live in the house next door, but when it became too crowded they moved to this house. Their former home is now occupied by two other people but she still does her cooking there because that house has a stove.

Basically, the house was an elongated rectangle divided into three square rooms set next to each other like boxes. In the center was the general living area, flanked on each side by a bedroom. The main room contained an old square table, some chairs, and very little else. Even though the house was rather new, there were stains on the walls, probably from water leaking in when it rained. Just about the only decoration on the walls was a portrait of Chairman Mao.

In the one bedroom I saw there was a wooden dresser, the top of which was covered with dozens of tiny family portraits. In a corner of the room stood a beautiful hand-carved bed that hinted at a period of affluence in the past. The woman explained that she and her husband had bought it when they were newly married. It was covered with an intricately crocheted spread.

Her children, she told us, ranged in ages from ten to nineteen. "In bringing up children," she said, "it is important to teach them something about history. I often tell them how much conditions have improved and how bitter things were in the past under the landlords."

This is a point the Chinese often make. Throughout our trip we were constantly being told about improvements in living conditions. In most cases I'm sure this talk is justified. Yet, when we said good-bye to this woman, I left the house wondering how her words could be reconciled with her hand-carved bed.

Entrance to a former landlord's house

"SPARKLING RED STAR"

That evening we were entertained with a private screening of the film "Sparkling Red Star," which was shown for us at the guesthouse where we were staying. The audience, in addition to myself, my brother, and our translator, included the Mexican couple and the guesthouse staff. Since the film was not dubbed and had no subtitles, the translator was kept busy providing us with a running translation. The movie employed sophisticated cinematographic techniques and obviously had been made quite recently, but its blatant propaganda message was pegged at so simple a level that one couldn't help thinking it had been made for children. Because it was such a novelty to us, and because we hadn't seen a movie in weeks, we found it rather entertaining, but I'm sure that if we ever had to sit through another one like it we would all fall asleep.

SU-CHOU CARVING FACTORY

Sunday morning we set off early for the Su-chou Carving Factory. Our guide for the tour was Mr. Wei, who welcomed us warmly and explained the history of the factory. When it was established in 1954, it employed only seven workers. By 1958 the number of workers had grown to over a hundred. "The number of workers tripled after the Great Leap Forward and then doubled again after the campaign to criticize Confucius and Lin Piao," Mr. Wei informed us, although he didn't explain what possible connection there could be between these political developments and the growth of a carving factory.

Our short briefing session concluded with Mr. Wei reminding us that this was a relatively new factory. "If you find any shortcomings and defects in management, or in our products," he said, "please feel free to point them out." Obviously, this statement could not be taken at face value. How could a couple of teenagers who knew nothing about the business spot any problems? In part the invitation was meant as a courtesy, and in part it was said to illustrate the humility of the Communist Chinese, who believe it is important to be willing to learn from anyone.

The carving factory makes two types of products—mahogany carving and lacquer carving. The mahogany carving ranges from small pieces such as cigarette boxes to larger pieces such as bookshelves and doors. Like most of the luxury goods manufactured in China, these products are largely for export, although some are sold to hotels in China.

Workers in the factory work a six-day week with Friday off. As our guide explained, "Factories all take different days off because if they all took their holiday at the same time the streets would be crowded with people." Of all the industries to which we had been introduced, the wood-carving business was the only one that actually had a formal apprenticeship system. Young workers must serve a three-year apprenticeship before they become full-fledged carvers earning a fixed salary. A twenty-year-old apprentice to whom we spoke told us that he had only six months to go in his apprenticeship.

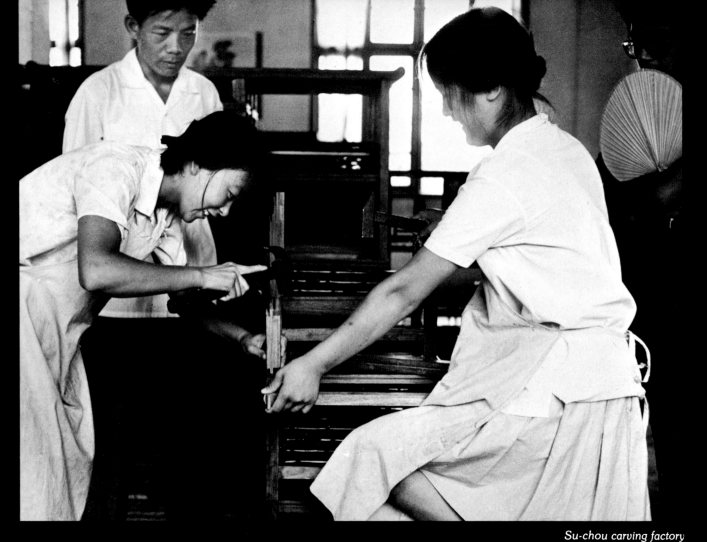

Su-chou carving factory

The streets of Su-chou

Late Sunday morning we boarded a train that would take us to Shanghai. I was looking forward with great anticipation to our visit there. This would be the first really large city we had seen since Peking. Besides, it was the only place in China I knew other than Peking, for we had stopped there briefly on our earlier visit with the party of President Marcos. And if that weren't enough reason to be excited, I was looking forward to our stay at the famous Peace Hotel, which was at one time one of the most splendid hotels in the Far East.

Since it was Sunday, we asked our guide Mr. Li if we could go to Mass. He told us it was out of the question. When we insisted, he went off to make inquiries. After a little while he returned and informed us that although he had managed to find a church, there was no priest. Under the circumstances, it didn't seem we had any choice.

Both Philip and I were rather exhausted after ten days of uninterrupted tourism. Few things, I suppose, are less relaxing than a vacation. In any case, we asked Mr. Li to cancel whatever excursions he had planned for us that afternoon. At that point we felt the best use we could make of our time would be to spend it recuperating in our room.

TAO-FU PEOPLE'S COMMUNE

On Monday morning we visited the Tao-Fu People's Commune. One of the smaller communes in the Shanghai area, it contains three townships with a total population of about 16,000. The main crops grown on its approximately 1,200 hectares of cultivated land are rice, wheat, and vegetables. Before the Liberation, 70 percent of the people in the area worked for the landlords or the rich capitalists. In 1949 a land reform program distributed the land among the people who tilled it. Unfortunately, this didn't work out very well because each farmer received only a tiny portion of land too small to support himself and his family. Then, in 1953, a new program of cooperative farming was instituted. Originally begun on a small scale with only twenty households, the cooperative system quickly grew, so that by 1956 between 300 and 400 households were participating members. By 1958 the agricultural co-op had evolved into the People's Commune.

The system of communal ownership has paid tremendous dividends for the people of the area, who all benefit from the dramatic increases in the productivity of the land. For example, in 1953 an average crop was approximately 3,000 kilograms of grain per hectare.

By 1974 this figure had almost quadrupled to 11,400 kilograms per hectare.

In addition to raising crops, the commune also has an animal husbandry program, a small forestry program, and a fishery. There is a machine shop for repairing farming equipment, a chemical factory that produces agricultural insecticides, a brickyard that manufactures bricks for local construction, and a grain processing plant. The spokesman who briefed us on the commune ended his presentation with the proud proclamation that "Our task here at the Tao-Fu People's Commune is five-fold. The five elements of our commune are agriculture, industry, commerce, education, and militia. In this way we are carrying out the principle of Chairman Mao, who says that although agriculture is primary, we must have an all-around development."

The improvements brought about in the field of education have been even more dramatic than the increases in agricultural productivity. Before the Liberation, the impoverished population of this area was almost completely illiterate. Today, thanks to a system of compulsory universal schooling, illiteracy has been completely eliminated in the younger generation, and many older people have learned to read and write.

Finally, the commune boasts an excellent health care system. One small hospital serves the whole commune, but every work brigade has its own medical service station and every production team has a case worker who makes regular house visits. A cooperative medical service system was initiated in 1969. Every member of the commune pays two *yuan* annually to support the system. This entitles him or her to see the doctor, to go to the hospital if necessary, and to receive any drugs that may be required at no additional charge. What is more, there are also a number of "barefoot doctors" who provide minor medical assistance to the members of the commune.

"The life of the people is now greatly improved, if we compare it to the conditions of the past," our guide concluded. "But if we compare it to the requirements of Chairman Mao, we can see that there is still the need for much development and there are many things that need to be improved. For example, the Fourth National Congress has set the target date of 1980 for the full mechanization of agriculture. Here at the commune we are hoping to achieve that goal by 1978."

We were fortunate enough to be able to interview some young members of the commune. We spoke to Miss Tsao, a twenty-four-year-old native of Shanghai who has been in the commune since 1969. Using the same phrase that practically all the other young people used, she told us that she had come to the countryside "to answer the call of Chairman Mao for young educated people to go to the countryside to be reeducated."

For the past few years she has served as the accountant of a work brigade. Because each brigade includes farms, factories, and businesses, a considerable amount of bookkeeping is necessary in

Commune dining hall

order to keep it going as a self-sustaining economic unit. Her heavy load of responsibilities as an accountant, however, does not exempt her from physical labor in the fields. She told us that she usually averages about ten days of work in the fields each month.

"Many young people," she told us, "come to the countryside each year. Some of them stay only a few years and then are transferred back to the factories or the university. But many of us have learned to love it here in the country and would prefer to stay. That is the way I feel. I am sure I could go back to the university to study some more, and when I first came here that is what I thought I would do. Because I grew up in Shanghai, I felt that I wanted to live in a big city. But now I have changed my mind. For me, the countryside is like one big university where there is so much to be learned and where the peasants are such good teachers."

We next spoke to Mr. Wong, who served as the chief of a production team. One of his main tasks, he told us, was to take care of the young people who are constantly arriving from the city. "Sometimes," he said, "it is not easy for them to learn to adjust to life in the country after having been raised in such a different environment. Although some of them have studied agricultural techniques in their school classes, they do not know how to go about applying their knowledge in practical situations. The peasants, too, have to be educated about farming, but for the opposite reason. They have their traditional ways of doing things, and must be trained in the new techniques of planting and harvesting that are necessary if we are to increase the productivity of the land. For all these reasons, we have established a system of study classes for the members of the commune. There are classes in agriculture and agricultural machinery for the peasants, and there are also classes in which the peasants teach the young people from the city. We also have ideological study classes in which both peasants and city youths read and discuss the writings of Marx, Lenin, and Chairman Mao. We even have invited teachers to come from the university to give lectures. And sometimes the peasants give lectures on the class system as it used to exist before the Liberation. It is very important for young people to learn about the past so that they can understand the significance of what we are doing today. My job as chief of a production brigade is to coordinate and organize these various education programs as well as to organize the production itself."

Before we began our tour of the commune itself, we were shown a miniature model of the entire area. It was a beautifully detailed piece of work, adorned with dozens of blinking lights like the running lights of a tiny airplane. Coded in different colors, the lights indicated various features of the commune. Our guide pointed out the nine schools, the seven irrigation stations, and the various clinics. I suspect that this exquisite little model had been given to the commune by one of its members, who built it in his spare time as a labor of love.

When we boarded our cars to begin our tour, the dark sky was threatening rain, which would have been a relief on this hot,

Our pleasant impression of the Commune was due in no small part to the contagious enthusiasm of this elderly woman

Laundry

muggy day. The air, however, was surprisingly still, stirred occasionally by a laconic breeze.

Our tour took us from the badly lit and cluttered machinery repair shop to the poultry farm, the pigsty, the dairy barn, and one of the many medical service stations. The medical station was staffed by five men who alternate tours of duty in the little one-room clinic with shifts in the field. The walls of the clinic were lined with jars of herbs. When I told the man on duty that I had a cold and asked if he could help, he disappeared into a large closet and reappeared a few minutes later with a couple of plastic-wrapped packages stamped with Chinese characters. The packages turned out to contain chrysanthemum tea, which I was told to take at every meal. Later that night I tried it in my hotel room. It was delicious tea, but if it had any medicinal value at all, my cold didn't seem to notice it.

The house we visited in the Tao-Fu Commune was almost identical to the one we stopped at in Su-chou. It too was a boxlike structure divided into thirds, with the main living area at the center. The lady of the house, who was gracious enough to invite us in and to answer our questions, told us that she lived there with her husband, her son, her daughter-in-law, and her grandson. The five of them had a combined annual income of 1,500 yuan. Although her family was by no means affluent, or even comfortable by Western standards, the woman was quite satisfied with their living conditions. "Before the Liberation," she explained, "my husband and I worked for the landlord. We did not have steady employment. Often there wasn't even enough money to buy rice, so we had to make do with just the husks of wheat. Back then, we lived in this very same house, only it has been rebuilt since the Liberation. When we first moved in, it was made of straw."

She was an elderly woman—I would guess in her sixties, although she did not tell us her age. She and her husband both worked in the fields, but their assignments were not very arduous. "Old people are given special consideration and are assigned only light duties," she informed us. She went on to point out that some of the families in the commune were financially much better off than hers. Her next door neighbors, for example, who were much younger and therefore able to do more work, earned as much as 2,600 yuan a year. Out of this they were able to save 1,600 yuan.

Over all, our impression of the Tao-Fu People's Commune was a very pleasant one, due in no small part to the contagious enthusiasm communicated by this elderly woman.

LU WAN CHILDREN'S PALACE

We had lunch in Shanghai that afternoon, and then, at about three o'clock, we were taken to visit the Lu Wan Children's Palace. This is a recreation center for primary school children between the ages of seven and thirteen. During the school year it is open only between

There was a sudden outburst of applause and cheering

A group of children put on a variety show for our benefit

three and five o'clock in the afternoon, but during the summer it is also open two additional hours in the morning. Anywhere from 800 to 1,000 children visit the Children's Palace every day.

As we entered the main door, we heard hundreds of little children singing, chanting, and clapping. Then the noise stopped abruptly, apparently on a signal we didn't see. After a few seconds of silence, there was a sudden outburst of applause and cheering. It took us a few moments to realize that it was for us. Mr. Shei, a member of the Children's Palace staff, stepped forward to greet us. "We will take a few minutes," he said, "to let our children tell you about their activities here."

On cue, a small girl in pigtails tied with dainty white ribbons stepped forward and recited loudly in a shrill, singsong voice. "How do you do, uncles?" she began. "We are very happy to welcome you to our Children's Palace. Allow me, on behalf of all the children, to extend to you our warmest welcome."

Uncles! As small as she was, we were not that much older than she was.

As soon as she finished speaking, she stepped back into the crowd of children and a second girl popped out like a jack-in-the-box. Gaily dressed in a loud print blouse and an even louder print skirt in a completely different pattern, she too recited a speech for us.

"The Children's Palace is a center where we children can carry on our activites outside of school. The name of this district palace is Lu Wan Children's Palace. There are many activities for us here. We also have study classes in which we can exchange our thoughts on the works of Chairman Mao. Because we study the works of Chairman Mao, we will learn how to serve the people and will be able to do something for old people. We have exercise classes and art classes and classes where we work at ship modeling, airplane modeling, and building radios. We also have sports and games and a shadow box theater. We have fun here and we also learn to understand the happiness which we have been given by the Party and Chairman Mao."

At the conclusion of this incredible speech, two children stepped forward and took my brother and me by the hand to lead us around the palace. In a small auditorium a group of children put on a variety show for our benefit. They sang and danced and played musical instruments. In another room we witnessed a performance of the shadow box theater and then were taken "backstage" to observe the children as they manipulated the countless wires that brought the little puppets to life. We saw workshops where boys and girls were building radios and working on models of airplanes and ships.

The end of our tour brought us to the main recreation room, which was so crowded with games of various descriptions that it looked like a penny arcade. On closer examination, however, it was apparent to us that all these games had been built by the children themselves. My brother and I were talked into competing with two twelve-year-olds in a stationary bicycle race. I'll leave it to the reader to guess who won.

Traffic tower, Shanghai

SHANGHAI DANCING SCHOOL

It took a lot of doing, but we managed to convince our guides to arrange a visit to the Shanghai Dancing School. This was one of the things I had put on the original typewritten list I gave to Mr. Li when we first arrived in China. He told me then that the members of the dancing school were often away on tour, and so there was a good chance that we would miss them. Besides, the school usually did not allow visitors, or at least did not encourage them.

We were in luck. Not only were we allowed to visit, but we were given a very warm welcome. As we drove up to the school, our guide pointed out a large board with cutout Chinese characters which he volunteered to translate for us. The sign said, "Welcome to our Filipino friends."

At the briefing session which always precedes tours in China, we learned that the Shanghai Dancing School had been founded in 1960. It was closed at the time of the Proletarian Cultural Revolution, but in 1971 it began accepting students again. In a sense, the name Shanghai Dancing School is a misnomer: It *is* a school, but it is also a professional dance troupe which tours the country, giving performances throughout China.

Students come from all over the country to study here. Tuition is free, and each student pays only four *yuan* a year for food. All other expenses, including clothing and dancing shoes, are supplied by the state. When a student graduates from the school and begins dancing in the troupe, he or she is paid wages of fifty-seven *yuan* a month. In all, there are about 700 students in the school, including slightly over a hundred from the first class that entered when the school reopened in 1971.

The troupe's most celebrated performance is a show known as the White Hericle Ballet. This is a dance drama in which workers, peasants, and soldiers are featured as the heroes. It is very popular in the countryside and has been filmed for showing on television and in theaters.

At the conclusion of the briefing session we were treated to a lengthy exhibition of the students' skills. The dance technique could probably best be described as a cross between traditional ballet and acrobatics. Not being a dance critic, I won't attempt to describe it, other than to say that the show put on for us included everything from dainty toe dancing to a vigorous session of tumbling on a mat spread out across the floor.

After the show, we had a meeting with about a dozen students. We asked some of them how they came to be students at the dancing school and got a number of interesting answers. An eighteen-year-old boy told us that he asked his teacher in middle school to recommend him for the dancing school after he saw a performance of the troupe and fell in love with the "Revolutionary ballet." Another told us that even as a small child he had always loved to perform and that his teachers in school knew it. They suggested that he apply for the ballet school and endorsed his application.

young people tell me that they had gone to work in the oil fields in answer to the call of Chairman Mao, and gone to live in a commune in answer to the call of Chairman Mao, and gone to the university in answer to the call of Chairman Mao, and left the university in answer to the call of Chairman Mao, I had had enough.

I wanted to grab one of them and shake him and say, "Stop it! You're a real person, just like I am. We all have to do some things because we should do them, whether we like it or not. But knowing that we should do it is not the same thing as liking it. Why can't you people see the difference? Have you never had a single selfish thought? Why do you pretend you are so much better than we are?"

Perhaps I was being a bit irrational. Perhaps I was being unfair to them. But on the other hand, perhaps I was being more fair to them than the system that taught them not to recognize their own desires, or even to acknowledge that they had desires.

Even after we left the dancing school, I couldn't shake off the depressing thoughts that our talk with the students had occasioned. I continued to brood about it as we walked down one of the main streets of Shanghai. Soon we found ourselves in the middle of a large shopping center where all the store fronts were decorated with large signs painted with Roman letters. In the mood I was in, this also bothered me. It seemed to me that the Roman letters spelling out the Chinese names phonetically were not at all natural, for the result was an overabundance of X's and unusual diphthongs. Besides, adoption of the Roman alphabet seemed inconsistent with the Chinese policy of minimizing Western influence. And how could such an orthographic reform possibly work in a country where dialect differences were so great that a person from one province often couldn't be understood in another province? For all its disadvantages, the use of Chinese characters at least allowed people throughout the country to communicate with each other by writing.

Be that as it may, I decided that the ruling powers must have had their reasons, and so I made a conscious effort to forget about it. Unfortunately, this was turning into the kind of day when it didn't seem that anything would go right. At a fruit stand only a few feet from where we were walking a scuffle suddenly broke out. Before long it looked like it was turning into a full-fledged fight. Our guide tried to tell us that it was of an ideological nature, but to my inexperienced eye it seemed more a case of a ripped-off melon.

Later that afternoon we boarded a plane for a flight to Ch'ang-sha. The sun was just setting as we touched down, and as we taxied toward the terminal I saw out the window a rather unsettling sight. Through open hangar doors I could see row after row of fighter planes. Somehow it gave me the feeling that I was seeing something I wasn't supposed to see. Philip and I exchanged glances and then stared out the window at them.

Looking back now, I don't know why I reacted that way. I am perfectly well aware that China is one of the world's major military powers. But for some reason the sight of all those predatory machines shattered my image of China as a big but impoverished agricultural nation, passive and fretfully pondering its defenses against the industrial giants.

Ch'ang-sha is a strangely lovely city. The capital of Hunan Province, it boasts a population of over a million but seems very much like a small town in the middle of a rural setting. All around the city, green rice fields stretch out toward the red clay hills.

The hotel where we stayed was one of the most paradoxical places I had ever seen. A huge building, it seemed to have been set down in the middle of nowhere and was surrounded entirely by barren fields. Basically, it was an old hotel with a couple of new wings, but even the new wings were so austere and unpretentious that they seemed practically squalid. The vast lobby reminded me of an unused gymnasium.

When I got to my room, I discovered it was already inhabited— by hundreds of the largest mosquitos I had ever seen. The windows had no screens, but I consoled myself with the observation that the four-poster bed was surrounded by a very effective-looking mosquito net. Later that night I was to learn that an effective mosquito net is not much good if the mosquitos are already on the inside. In effect, the mosquitos and I spent the night locked up together in a gauze cage. The only purpose of the net, I think, was to save the mosquitos the trouble of having to look for me.

THE BIRTHPLACE OF CHAIRMAN MAO

The first thing on our schedule Wednesday morning was a two-hour trip by car to Shao-shan. The long drive through rich farmland had a tranquilizing effect on me and gave me a chance to do some thinking. I realized I had been getting increasingly irritable the last few days and was annoyed with myself for it. I also realized that at least in part my petulance was a defensive reaction to China. The world that the Chinese young people lived in was so radically different from my own that it raised unsettling thoughts, calling into question all the values that I had automatically accepted as right up to now.

As the car sped on, cruising comfortably past the green rice fields sunk below the level of the roadway, it began to dawn on me

146

The long drive through rich farmland had a tranquilizing effect on me

that my annoyance with the dancing school students the day before may well have been the product of my own uncertainty. After all, who was I to criticize? The people—who are certainly the only ones qualified to judge—appeared to be genuinely and sincerely happy with the lives they led. The fact that I wouldn't have been happy under the same circumstances suddenly seemed very much beside the point. It was an unsettling thought, but somehow I found my confusion almost refreshing, for it seemed to free me from the necessity of always passing judgment on China. Up to now I had been unconsciously assuming that the Chinese system and the system of values I lived by contradicted each other, so that if one of them was right, then the other had to be wrong. But in reality it wasn't that simple. It wasn't a matter of black and white. The two ways of life were alternatives; each had its pitfalls that the other avoided, each had its advantages.

Our arrival in Shao-shan put an end to my inner debate before I had a chance to reach any final conclusions. We were greeted warmly by a middle-aged official of the local tourist office, who in turn introduced us to the guide who would be conducting us around for the length of our short stay. What a delightful surprise! She was one of the prettiest girls I had seen since we first arrived in China. It was almost as though Fate or the government had been reading my mind and was now rewarding me for adopting a more positive attitude.

She took us first to the guesthouse where we were to stay. We left our belongings and stopped long enough for tea and cold towels. Then she led us on a pleasant walk through Shao-shan to a farmhouse on the outskirts of town—one of the major tourist attractions in all of China. It was here that Mao Tse-tung was born and raised. Along the way we passed a group of children playing on an embankment that led down to one of the rice fields. Attracted by the sight of foreign faces, they turned to us and waved cheerfully. The attitude of all the Chinese we met in this area contrasted sharply with what we had become used to. They were so unawed by my brother's camera that some of them even struck poses when they saw it pointed in their direction. One or two of them actually asked to have their pictures taken!

The house itself was surprisingly large, for I suppose I had expected Chairman Mao to have had the humblest origin. In fact, however, his father was a fairly well-to-do farmer. Although hardly opulent by any standards, it was a sturdy, well-built, and attractive yellow brick house that was made to seem even more appealing than it was by the storybook setting in which it was placed. It was tucked comfortably in a tiny valley formed by the lush green hills that rose all around it, and it seemed hardly possible that such a serene and peaceful spot could have given birth to thoughts of revolution. A small stream, crowded with water lilies, wandered down from the hills and crossed in front of the house. A primitive stone bridge arched over it.

The pilgrimage to Shao-shan

Some of them even struck poses ➡

Attracted by the sight of foreign faces, they turned to us and waved cheerfully

A large plaque over the doorway announces that this is the birthplace of Chairman Mao. Other than that, the house is identical to the way it was when Mao was growing up. I say "identical" because the original house was burned to the ground by the Kuomintang, so that the building we were now entering was actually a replica dating from after the Revolution.

Inside, the rooms were so dark that it was difficult to see for quite some time. There was so little furniture that at first I assumed that the government hadn't replaced the furnishings when the house was restored. Our guide, however, assured us that what we were seeing was a faithful copy of the way the interior looked in Chairman Mao's youth. Chinese farmers—even moderately well-to-do ones—apparently think of their houses as little more than places for eating and sleeping. Indeed, the only signs of luxury anywhere in the house were the rich mahogany four-poster beds, which looked like they must have been quite comfortable.

On one of the walls was a hook for an oil lamp, "where as a child he studied." Another wall held a small collection of family photographs. I found it almost impossible to believe that the tall, slender young man standing with his family in one of the pictures was the same person I had seen depicted in thousands of portraits and statues all over China. In the picture before me he was wearing the traditional clothing of the countryside, which made him look rather like a priest.

Toward the back of the house we found the simple kitchen which, I was surprised to see, did not contain a stove. When I commented on this, our guide took us to another room to show us the stove. Because it was the only source of heating in the house, the family had wisely decided not to waste its warmth on the kitchen.

We left through a side door that opened into a narrow courtyard where the livestock used to be kept. Unused farm implements lay on the ground and stood against the walls.

After our walk back to Shao-shan, we were taken to a large squarish building just off the black-asphalt-covered town square. The building turned out to be a museum of the life of Chairman Mao, and we were obliged to listen to a long and excruciatingly boring lecture that wasn't helped any by the fact that we had to sit through it twice—once while the museum guide rambled on and on in Chinese, and then a second time when our translator rendered her speech into English. I guess they could see how bored we were, because after a while they brought in stools for us to sit on. But they didn't shorten the lecture and I'm positive that not even the tiniest detail of Mao's life was left out.

We had lunch in the guesthouse and then were driven to the airport for the flight to Canton—the last leg of our travels through China.

The birthplace of Chairman Mao

In Canton we stayed at a hotel for foreigners directly across from the Canton Fair Exhibition Hall. We woke up Thursday morning to a day of beautiful sunshine, and right after breakfast were taken to tour a number of parks and gardens. One of them was called "Seventy-two Mothers Park," to commemorate the mothers of some heroes who were killed in the Revolution. The fact that the park was named for the mothers instead of the heroes themselves intrigued me, but our guide didn't offer much in the way of explanation.

We noticed that the parks and the streets of Canton were filled with visiting Chinese from Hong Kong. It seemed to me that the people of Canton, whom we found to be quite warm and friendly, treated the visitors from Hong Kong with a coldness that bordered on hostility.

FU-SAN PORCELAIN WORKS

In the afternoon we drove from Canton to nearby Fu-san. On our way out of Canton, we were stopped at the city limits and had to show exit permits allowing us to leave the city. I imagine the Chinese feel that this extra bit of security is required because of the close proximity of Hong Kong, which is of course politically independent of China.

Fu-san is the center of the porcelain industry in China and we had asked specifically to go there in order to have a chance to tour one of the factories. Unfortunately, our visit was disappointing. Although the factory was modern and well run, and although it produced beautiful porcelainware, there was nothing unique or interesting about it. Except for the fact that the workers looked Chinese, we could have been anywhere in the world.

THE PEOPLE'S LIBERATION ARMY

When we returned to Canton, our guide jubilantly announced that she had succeeded in arranging for us to interview a group of soldiers from the People's Liberation Army. We had been asking for such an interview since we first arrived in China and all along had been told that it would not be possible.

The meeting was held in a private room off the lobby of our hotel. The army contingent consisted of about half a dozen young soldiers and two older men who were obviously superior officers, although their uniforms were not adorned with any insignia of rank that we could detect. We began by asking them how they had come to be in the army.

One of the older men explained that membership in the People's Liberation Army is strictly voluntary. Indeed, a person does not get to be a soldier simply by voluntarily signing up. He must also

A Canton street

be
is r
req
pas
one
"It
forr
sati
nec

us
sho
pro
tha
"W
hap
off,
tha
aga
grac
help

adju
que
con
rais
too

con
that
for
we
sold
arm
Con
stud

the
and
in t
is n
mili
phy
affa
we

five
ther
to s
trai

Fu-san Porcelain Works

explanation difficult to believe. "Yes, we do," he said. "But you must understand that politically a general is on exactly the same level as a soldier. The difference is only one of position. I do not know how to explain it to you any better. The general's job is to command the soldier, and the soldier's job is to obey. In that sense, the general's job is superior to the soldier's job. But the general himself is not superior to the soldier. Perhaps you think it comes to the same thing, but I assure you it does not."

I found his explanation entirely convincing—all the more so because it came from one of the younger men rather than from either of the two I had taken to be officers. The rest of our talk passed quite pleasantly and we discussed many inconsequential things. For a while the soldiers questioned my brother and me about life in the Philippines. Like most of the Chinese we had talked with, they were especially curious about our schooling.

Finally, it was time for the meeting to break up. We thanked them warmly for giving so much time to us and asked if we could prevail upon them for one more favor. We wanted to hear them sing one of their army songs.

They seemed flattered by the request, which they discussed among themselves for a few minutes. Then Comrade Yen informed us that they had selected "Heroes from the Hill." He began by himself, singing in a loud voice, and was quickly joined by the others. Although we couldn't understand a word of the lyrics, the impact of the stirring anthem was by no means lost on us. As they sang, I realized with mixed feelings of longing and regret that within a few hours we would be boarding an airplane for the flight home to Manila. Somehow the thought forced me to listen all the more intently to the song, for it seemed to me that in the soaring voices of these young soldiers I was hearing the voice of China.